FEAR NOT!

Kara Eckmann

Gospel Light

Gospel Light is an evangelical Christian publisher dedicated to serving the local church. We believe God's vision for Gospel Light is to provide church leaders with biblical, user-friendly materials that will help them evangelize, disciple and minister to children, youth and families.

We hope this Gospel Light resource will help you discover biblical truth for your own life and help you minister to youth. God bless you in your work.

For a free catalog of resources from Gospel Light please contact your Christian supplier or call 1-800-4-GOSPEL.

PUBLISHING STAFF
William T. Greig, Publisher
Dr. Elmer L. Towns, Senior Consulting Publisher
Dr. Gary S. Greig, Senior Consulting Editor
Jean Daly, Managing Editor
Pam Weston, Editorial Assistant
Kyle Duncan, Associate Publisher
Bayard Taylor, M.Div., Editor, Theological and Biblical Issues
Debi Thayer, Designer

ISBN 0-8307-1823-0
© 1997 Gospel Light
All rights reserved.
Printed in U.S.A.

How to Make Clean Copies from This Book

You may make copies of portions of this book with a clean conscience if:

- you (or someone in your organization) are the original purchaser;
- you are using the copies you make for a noncommercial purpose (such as teaching or promoting your ministry) within your church or organization;
- you follow the instructions provided in this book.

However, it is **ILLEGAL** for you to make copies if:

- you are using the material to promote, advertise or sell a product or service other than for ministry fund-raising;
- you are using the material in or on a product for sale;
- you or your organization are **not** the original purchaser of this book.

By following these guidelines you help us keep our products affordable.
Thank you,
Gospel Light

Permission to make photocopies or to reproduce by any other mechanical or electronic means in whole or in part of any designated* page, illustration or activity in this book is granted only to the original purchaser and is intended for noncommercial use within a church or other Christian organization. None of the material in this book may be reproduced for any commercial promotion, advertising or sale of a product or service. Sharing of the material in this book with other churches or organizations not owned or controlled by the original purchaser is also prohibited. All rights reserved.

*Pages with the following notation can be legally reproduced:

© 1997 by Gospel Light. Permission to photocopy granted.

CONTENTS

HOW TO USE *FEAR NOT!*

This 5 to 10-session course is designed to help junior high students explore who God is and why they can trust Him for everything.

During this course students will discover or review that faith in God means...

- believing God is in control and will take care of us;
- being aware of His presence;
- acting in obedience to God in all situations;
- knowing that God loves and accepts all people;
- accepting God's love and forgiveness.

You can use *Fear Not!* for Vacation Bible School, camp or retreat—or your regular youth fellowship meetings any time of the year. *Fear Not!* is designed to be a flexible course with the ability to expand from 5 to 10 sessions.

ABOUT INVOLVEMENT LEARNING

So often we hear or read accounts of youth who live empty lives and have no apparent goals or direction in life. To fill the emptiness, they often turn to activities that ultimately only heighten that emptiness. Now more than ever, today's youth need to know that the potential to live this dynamic kind of life is firmly rooted in the study of and obedience to God's Word.

It takes courage to live an obedient life and it takes strength to overcome the many barriers to Christian growth erected by the world. Therefore, it is not enough to simply tell today's youth that studying and obeying God's Word will lead to a productive life. Many teachers have helped their youth know this truth for themselves through involvement learning.

The teaching methods and materials in this book emphasize involvement learning. These methods will involve your students in the learning process and take them from the role of passively listening to one of actively digging into the Scriptures. These methods will help you create in your students the desire to examine God's Word and to make practical applications of the truths being studied.

Each session in this study includes three activities for each session:

- **Approach to the Word**—involves students in activities that capture and direct their interest toward the theme of the session.
- **Bible Exploration**—students use a variety of methods to learn what the Bible says about the session's theme.

- **Conclusion and Decision**—involves each student in a discussion or activity that provides a way to apply the Bible truths to his or her own life.

Within each session is an option to expand the session to two meetings, making a total of 10 sessions. If you are using the 5-session track, the following note gives you the directions at the end of the Bible Exploration:

Note: If you are completing this session in one meeting, ignore this break and continue on to "Conclusion and Decision."

Immediately following this **Note** you will find directions for expanding to a 10-session study:

Two-Meeting Track: If you want to spread this session over two meetings, STOP here and close in prayer. Inform students of the content to be covered in your next meeting.

The **Two-Meeting Track** box is then followed by:
- **Review and Approach**—gives an opportunity for review of the previous lesson and an introduction to the Bible Exploration #Two;
- **Bible Exploration Two**—further expands on the Bible study of the previous session.

The ideas provided in these sessions may stimulate additional ideas of your own which fit your group and teaching style. It is our prayer that the learning experiences suggested in this book, coupled with the power of God's Word, will challenge and motivate your students—encouraging some to become Christians and stirring up those who have grown complacent in their spiritual lives.

INTRODUCING YOUNG PEOPLE TO CHRIST

How do you present Christ to a young person?

1. **Pray.** Ask God to prepare the hearts of students to receive the message and prepare you to present it.

2. **Lay the foundation.** Youth are evaluating you and the Lord you serve by everything you do and say. They are looking for people in whose lives knowing God makes a noticeable difference, for people who love them and listen to them—the same way God loves them and listens to them.

   Learn to listen with your full attention. Learn to share honestly both the joys and the struggles you encounter as a Christian. Be honest about your own questions and about your personal concern for students. Learn to accept teens as they are. Christ died for them while they were yet sinners. You are also called to love them as they are.

3. **Be aware of opportunities.** A student may ask to talk after class. Or some might be waiting for you to suggest going for a soda—getting alone together where you can share what Jesus Christ means to you.

4. **Have a plan.** Don't lecture or force the issue. Here are some tips to keep in mind:

   - **Put the student at ease.** Be perceptive of feelings and remember he or she is probably nervous. Be relaxed, natural and casual in your conversation, not critical or judgmental.

   - **Get the student to talk**, and listen carefully to what is said. Students sometimes make superficial or shocking statements just to get your reaction. Don't begin lecturing or problem-solving. Instead encourage him or her to keep talking.

   - **Be gently direct.** Students may have trouble bringing up the topic. If you sense this, a simple question like, "How are you and God getting along?" can unlock a life-changing conversation.

   - **Discuss God's desire to have fellowship with people.** As you relate the plan God has for enabling people to have a relationship with Him, move through the points slowly enough to allow time for thinking and comprehending. However, do not drag out the presentation:
     a. God's goal for us is abundant life (see John 3:16, 10:10).
     b. All people are separated from God by sin (see Romans 3:23; 6:23).

  c. God's solution is Jesus Christ who died to pay the penalty for our sin (see Romans 5:8; John 14:6).

  d. Our response is to receive Christ as Savior (see John 1:12).

- **Make sure the student understands that accepting Christ is very simple,** though very profound. If you feel the student understands, ask if he or she would like to accept Christ now. If so, ask the student to pray with you. Explain that praying is simply talking to God. In this case it's telling God of the student's need for Christ and desire for Christ to be in his or her life as personal Lord and Savior. Then suggest that the student study in order to begin growing in the faith.

  If the student feels unready to make a decision, suggest some Scripture to read and make an appointment to get together again. John 14—16, Romans 3—8 and the Gospel of Mark are good sections of Scripture for reading. Pray for the student in the meantime.

5. **Remember your responsibility is simply to present the gospel** and to be able to explain the hope that is within you. It is the Holy Spirit who makes the heart ready for a relationship with God and gives growth.

WHEN IT'S ALL SAID AND DONE

When it's all said and done, what is done will far outlast what is said.

The time you invest in building relationships, encouraging and affirming students, listening to them and putting up with their rowdy moods (which seem to be never ending) will pay dividends in the Kingdom of God.

It is the personal touch that does it. Kids know when someone cares for them. It shows. It pays off. It declares loudly, "Here is a real person who has a real relationship with Christ, who wants to know the real you."

Relationships should not end with the packing away of materials. New contacts have been made during these days. These contacts need to be followed up.

Plan follow-up for those who become Christians. Get them into Sunday School. Visit their homes to answer questions and give encouragement. Provide transportation when needed.

Plan follow-up for those who rededicate their lives to the Lord. They need guidance in Bible study, in prayer and in preparing for the work the Lord has for them.

Plan follow-up for the unsaved. Invite them to church youth activities. Bring them to Sunday School and worship services. Continue to pray for them by name and keep in touch with them. Remember birthdays with a card or phone call.

Plan follow-up for unchurched parents. Show genuine interest in their young people. Continue to invite the entire family to church services and church activities—especially to adult Bible classes.

And when that once ornery student begins to respond to the love and caring you have shown, don't be surprised if he or she thinks about you and what you did to demonstrate God's love—and then tries to do the same for someone else.

COURAGEOUS CROSSING:

MOSES' FAITH SAVES THE ISRAELITES

KEY VERSES

"Moses answered the people, 'Do not be afraid. Stand firm and you will see the deliverance the LORD will bring you today. The Egyptians you see today you will never see again. The LORD will fight for you; you need only to be still.'" Exodus 14:13,14

"'The LORD is my strength and my song; he has become my salvation. He is my God, and I will praise him, my father's God, and I will exalt him.'" Exodus 15:2

BIBLICAL BASIS

Exodus 13:17—15:6

FOCUS OF THE SESSION

Faith is believing God is in control and will take care of us.

AIMS OF THIS SESSION

During this session students will:
- Examine the courage and faith of Moses and the Israelites;
- Discover that they can have confidence in the fact that God is sovereign and caring;
- Identify one specific area of their lives that they choose to release control to God.

LEADER'S DEVOTIONAL

Mission impossible! Surely that's what Moses must have thought. He was a new and insecure leader. He was placed in charge of over two million people. He had a faraway destination in the Promised Land.

But Moses had more than just enormous responsibilities; he also had faith that God was in control and would take care of His people. After all, he had just seen God show up in several ways: the burning bush, the ten plagues, Passover.

Has God changed since the time of Moses? No, He is the great unchanging I AM. He is still in control and cares for you and your students.

Have we lost sight of who God is? Yes, we have.

Think back on your own life. Think back over your last year. Think back on the toughest parts of your life. God was there, wasn't He? He works all things together for the good of those who love Him. You can have faith that God loves you. It is this trust that allows you and your students to release control of your lives to God.

If you or your students are in a tug-of-war with God, let go of the rope. You won't be a loser, but a winner!

APPROACH THE WORD (15 MINUTES)

Objective: To help students identify who is truly powerful.

Materials needed: Several copies of current magazines or newspapers. If there is no bulletin board available, provide a large sheet of poster board, newsprint or butcher paper on which to pin, staple or tape the pictures.

Divide students into groups of five. Explain: **Today we're going to talk about power. I am giving each group a stack of magazines and newspapers. Your goal is to tear out pictures of powerful people in these newspapers and magazines.** Before they begin, you may want to brainstorm for a few minutes some of the different types of powerful people: e.g. actors, politicians, singers, models and sports heroes.

After the groups have spent four to five minutes searching for and tearing out pictures of powerful people, each group will share who they have found as they attach their pictures to the bulletin board, poster board, newsprint or butcher paper that you have provided.

Discuss the following questions:

Why did you label these people as powerful?
Of all of these people, who is the most powerful?
In what situations might this person be powerless?

Make a transition to the lesson by saying: **Today we're going to examine the most powerful being in the whole universe, God. His power is never limited. Our faith is strengthened as we realize that God is in control and will take care of us.**

BIBLE EXPLORATION (45 MINUTES)

Objective: To allow students to look closely at God's sovereign control over Moses and the Israelites.

Materials needed: Enough copies of "Pictures of Power" on pages 19-21 for each student to have one, an overhead projector and a transparency of "Perfect Power" on pages 22-23 (if you do not have access to an overhead projector, you will need to provide each student with a copy of the "Perfect Power" handout), pencils and Bibles.

Step 1: With the whole group, read Exodus 14:8-28 aloud. You may want to have students take turns doing the reading. One way to divide up the verses is to number students from 8 to 28 (some students may get two or even three numbers, depending on the size of your group). Each student reads the verse that corresponds with his or her assigned number (i.e., Student Number Eight reads verse 8).

Step 2: Distribute a copy of "Pictures of Power" and a pencil to each student. Explain: **Today you have the chance to draw pictures of power described in the Bible.** Give them 15 minutes to draw their pictures.

Step 3: Have each student share what his or her favorite picture is. After each student shares, ask him or her: **What does this picture tell you about God's power?**

Step 4: Using the overhead transparency, follow the instructions on the "Perfect Power" handout. Work through the four statements with students, asking them if and how they need to be changed.

Note: If you are completing this session in one meeting, ignore this break and continue on to "Conclusion and Decision."

Two-Meeting Track: If you want to spread this session over two meetings, STOP here and close in prayer. Inform students of the content to be covered in your next meeting.

REVIEW AND APPROACH (10 MINUTES)

Objective: To trigger students' memories about Moses' faith and challenge them to think about who is truly powerful.

Materials needed: None.

Ask: **Today we're going to talk about power. If you had all the power in the world, what would you do? I'm going to read the following statements and you raise your hand to indicate which type of power you'd rather have.** Pause after each statement to give them time to respond.

Would you rather have the power to...

Get rid of all homework?	or	Get rid of all housework?
Go surfing next Saturday?	or	Go snow skiing next Saturday?
Be a star athlete?	or	Be a star student?
Find a way to abolish hunger?	or	Rid the world of hatred?
Develop a cure for AIDS?	or	Be able to stop all child abuse?

Then discuss the following:

Who do you consider to be powerful?

In general, do you feel very powerful? Why or why not?

What do you remember about the last session and the presence of God's power in Moses' life?

Make a transition to the lesson by saying: **Today we're going to dive deeper into this amazing story that reveals God's incredible power.**

BIBLE EXPLORATION TWO (45 MINUTES)

Objective: To help students examine what might have happened if God hadn't been in control of the Israelites' circumstances.

Materials needed: Enough copies of "Total Control" on page 24 and "Sing-Along" on page 25 for each student to have one of each, pens or pencils and Bibles.

Step 1: Explain: **In the story of Moses' and the Israelites crossing of the Red Sea, we can see God's total control over the situation.** Divide students into groups of four or five. Give each student a copy of "Total Control" and a pen or pencil. Allow 15 to 20 minutes for them to complete the handout.

Step 2: Discuss:

Do you think the Israelites realized that God was in control and cared for them? Explain.

How did this affect their faith?

Step 3: Give each student a copy of "Sing-Along." Ask everyone to work on it individually. As the leader you may need to give an example of how the blanks might be filled.

Step 4: After giving students 5 to 10 minutes to complete their handouts, lead a group prayer, asking each student to read his or her own personal versions of Exodus 15:2 as prayers of praise.

CONCLUSION AND DECISION (15 MINUTES)

Objective: To give students an opportunity to think about God's sovereign control over their own lives.

Materials needed: None.

Explain: **Right now we're going to take a "Power Walk." A power walk is a short walk around the church campus (or neighborhood if possible). During this walk, you are to do two things: First, remain totally silent. In other words, no talking. Second, look for examples of**

God's power. You may be reminded of God's power by seeing flowers or cars or people. The sky's the limit!

After their five-minute walk, ask:

What evidence did you see of God's power?

Why does the evidence you observed display God's power to you?

How can we be more aware of God's power every day?

Close in prayer, asking God to help you and your students see God's power every day.

ALTERNATE CONCLUSION (15 MINUTES)

Objective: To help students decide one area in their own lives that they need to turn over to God this week.

Materials needed: Paper, pens or pencils, and a bucket or box.

Divide your group into groups of five students each. Explain: **In your small groups, share your answers to the following questions** (Write them on the board, flip chart or overhead):

1. **In what ways have you seen God's power at work in your own life?**

2. **In what area(s) of your life do you sometimes forget that God's in control?**

3. **What is one way that you can trust in God's power more during the coming week?**

4. **What difference would turning control of this area over to God make in your life?**

After 10 minutes of small group discussion, give a piece of paper and a pen or pencil to each student. Explain: **I'll give you one minute to write down on this piece of paper one area of your life that you would like to give God control over.** After they have done so, explain: **This bucket at the front of the class represents God. If you want to give God control in that area of your life, come up to the bucket at the front of the class and place your piece of paper in the bucket, but only do it if you mean it.** You may want to go first in order to set an example for your students.

Close in prayer, asking God to help your students learn to turn control of their lives over to God.

PICTURES OF POWER

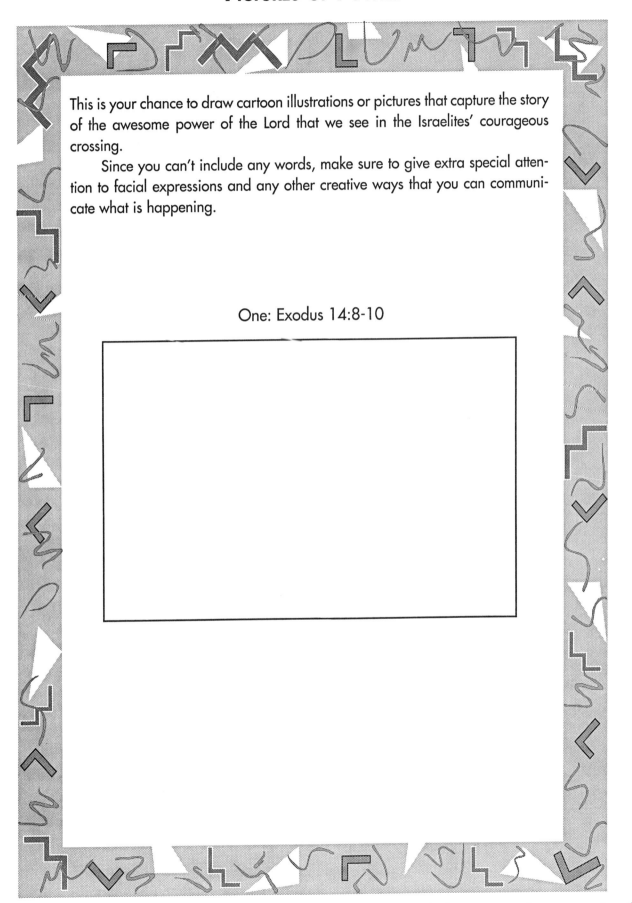

This is your chance to draw cartoon illustrations or pictures that capture the story of the awesome power of the Lord that we see in the Israelites' courageous crossing.

Since you can't include any words, make sure to give extra special attention to facial expressions and any other creative ways that you can communicate what is happening.

One: Exodus 14:8-10

CONTINUED

Two: Exodus 14:15-18

Three: Exodus 14:19-22

CONTINUED

Four: Exodus 14:23-25

Five: Exodus 14:26-28

PERFECT POWER

We've seen examples of God's power when He brought the Israelites across the Red Sea. Decide whether these statements describe God's power perfectly. If they don't, make whatever changes are needed to make them correct.

1. God is not involved much in human events.

2. God's power is enormous.

CONTINUED

3. Humans can predict whatever God is going to do.

4. Almost everything is under God's control.

TOTAL CONTROL

Read Exodus 13:17-22 to see how God *was* in total control.
List at least three examples of God's control in this passage.

1. _____

2. _____

3. _____

Imagine if God had not been in total control. What would have been different for the Israelites in Exodus 13:17—14:28? Draw at least three things.

SING-ALONG

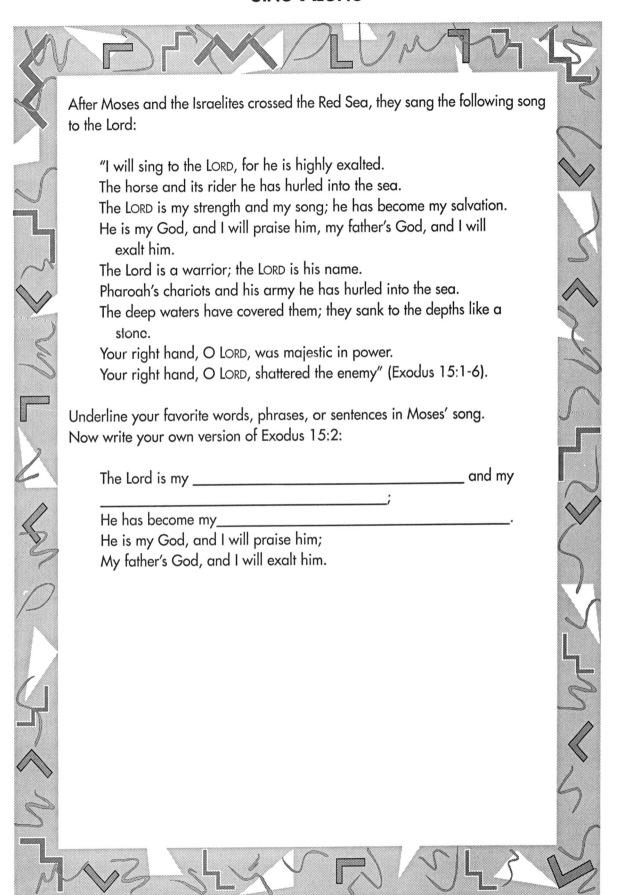

After Moses and the Israelites crossed the Red Sea, they sang the following song to the Lord:

"I will sing to the LORD, for he is highly exalted.
The horse and its rider he has hurled into the sea.
The LORD is my strength and my song; he has become my salvation.
He is my God, and I will praise him, my father's God, and I will
    exalt him.
The Lord is a warrior; the LORD is his name.
Pharoah's chariots and his army he has hurled into the sea.
The deep waters have covered them; they sank to the depths like a
    stone.
Your right hand, O LORD, was majestic in power.
Your right hand, O LORD, shattered the enemy" (Exodus 15:1-6).

Underline your favorite words, phrases, or sentences in Moses' song.
Now write your own version of Exodus 15:2:

The Lord is my _____ and my
_____;
He has become my_____.
He is my God, and I will praise him;
My father's God, and I will exalt him.

THE INVISIBLE ARMY:

ELISHA TRUSTS GOD

KEY VERSES

"And Elisha prayed, 'O LORD, open his eyes so he may see.' Then the LORD opened the servant's eyes, and he looked and saw the hills full of horses and chariots of fire all around Elisha. After they entered the city, Elisha said, 'LORD, open the eyes of these men so they can see.' Then the LORD opened their eyes and they looked, and there they were, inside Samaria." 2 Kings 6:17, 20

BIBLICAL BASIS

2 Kings 6:8-23; Hebrews 11:1

FOCUS OF THE SESSION

Faith is being aware of God's presence.

AIMS OF THIS SESSION

During this session the students will:
* Examine the benefits of Elisha's trust in God.
* Discover their need to trust in God alone.
* Implement a decision to trust in God in one area of their lives this week.

LEADER'S DEVOTIONAL

It's Sunday morning and Megan and her family are in their family station wagon on their way to church. As they drive into the parking lot, Megan sees her three closest friends Tori, Andrea and Jessica stepping out of Jessica's minivan. Tori and Andrea are carrying their sleeping bags and overnight suitcases. Apparently, Tori, Andrea and Jessica had a slumber party last night, but did not bother to invite Megan. If you were Megan, how would you feel?

It's Monday morning and Chris is heading for his locker to pick up his math book before first period. Two of the most popular guys in the eighth grade, Mike and Andy, are walking behind Chris. Thinking Chris can't hear them, they begin to criticize Chris's new haircut. Chris can hear them, but he doesn't know if he should turn around or keep walking. If you were Chris, how would you feel?

Situations such as these happen not just to Megan on Sunday and Chris on Monday; they happen to most junior highers just about every day. Most junior highers feel pretty insecure in their friendships and unsure of who they really are and who they want to be. For decades, junior high has been labeled a time of storm and stress, and rightly so. Junior highers can feel like they're drowning in a storm of hormones, emotions, humiliation and chaos.

The only real refuge from the storms of junior high life is found in the Lord. For students to survive and thrive in junior high, they *must* know that God is with them. He is present with them, not just in the past or the future, but in this very moment. It is this knowledge of God's presence that helps junior highers walk with a bit more self-confidence, and more importantly a ton of God-confidence. In the midst of disintegrating friendships and interpersonal awkwardness, junior highers need to cling to the truth of this lesson: God is all around them. In the midst of their storms, He is the only surefire life preserver.

APPROACH THE WORD (15 MINUTES)

Objective: To guide students into an understanding of the need to be aware of what is going on around them.

Preparation and materials needed: A video tape, TV set and VCR, paper and pens or pencils. Ahead of time, find a five-minute clip of a video that would be appropriate to show to your junior highers. (Hint: When in doubt, Disney cartoons work well!) Watch the clip and jot down 5 to 10 trivia questions about what happened in the video to ask students after they view it. You may want to have a small prize, such as a candy bar, for the winner of this video trivia contest.

Explain: **Today we're going to see how aware you are of what you see. I'm going to play this video tape and I want you to try to answer questions about what you saw.** While the tape is playing, pass out a paper and a pen or pencil to each student.

After viewing the five-minute clip, ask students the trivia questions that you prepared ahead of time. Have them work by themselves without helping one another. Read the answers out loud. Congratulate the winner.

Make a transition to the Bible Exploration by saying: **We often don't notice what is going on around us. I wonder how much we notice what God, who is always around us, is doing. Have you ever seen evidence of God working around you? How do you know He is with you?** Encourage discussion for a few minutes.

Then say: **Today we're going to see how being aware of God's presence is critical to our faith.**

BIBLE EXPLORATION (40 MINUTES)

Objective: To explore Elisha's faith in our invisible God.

Materials needed: Enough copies of "The Write Stuff" on pages 34-36 for each student to have one, Bibles, pens or pencils, and one piece of wood approximately three feet long.

Step 1: Make sure each student has a Bible. Explain: **You will be amazed by the story we're studying today. Let's turn together to 2 Kings 6:8-23. I'd like some volunteers to take turns reading the story aloud.** Try to get an equal number of male and female volunteers so they can alternate between male and female readers as they read the passage verse by verse.

Step 2: Divide your students into groups of four or five. Distribute a copy of "The Write Stuff" and a pen or pencil to each student. Explain: **Now you have a chance to pretend you are one of the characters actually watching what happened. You are to choose two of the following four characters—Elisha, the King of Israel, the King of Aram, or one of the soldiers of Aram—and answer the questions on the handout as if you were writing a letter to your best friend describing the event.** Give them about 10 minutes (or less if they seem to finish sooner) to complete the handout.

Step 3: Ask each group to read their two letters out loud to the entire class. Discuss the following:
What are some of the similarities between the letters?
What do these letters tell us about faith?

Step 4: Explain: **Often trusting in God means taking a big step. In fact, it often means you take a big step without knowing for certain where your foot is going to land. You simply have to believe that God is good and will take care of you even though you're in a tough or scary situation.**

I'm going to lay this piece of wood on the floor right here in the front of the room. As you are doing so, continue: **If you want to decide today to make the big step and trust God, here's what you can do today. Come to the front of the room and stand on the wood. Either out loud or to yourself, say, "God, this week I'm going to trust you by _____(fill in the blank)_____." Then take a step off the wood.**

You may want to demonstrate this yourself to give students an idea of what you're asking them to do.

> **Note:** If you are completing this session in one meeting, ignore this break and continue with "Conclusion and Decision."

> **Two-Meeting Track:** If you want to spread this session over two meetings, **STOP** here and close in prayer. Inform students of the content to be covered in your next meeting.

REVIEW AND APPROACH (15 MINUTES)

Objective: To trigger students' memories about the importance of being aware of what is both visible and invisible around them.

Materials needed: Bibles.

Explain: **Today we're going to begin with a little game. First, everyone find a partner.** Pause to allow them time to find a partner. Continue: **You and your partner should stand back to back, so that you can't see each other.** Pause. **When I say "turn," turn around, step back one step and look at your partner for five seconds. At the end of five seconds, return to your back-to-back position.** Ask: **Do you all understand? OK, ready, turn!**

Count to five out loud and then make sure all of the pairs return to their back-to-back positions. Explain: **Okay, now we're going to do a little "awareness test." Each one of you should make a minor change to your appearance, such as taking off your watch, or untying your shoelaces. Once each of you has done that, raise your hand.** Once you see that all of the students have their hands raised indicating that they have changed their appearance, say: **Okay, now when I say "turn," turn around and look at your partner for five seconds, trying to figure out what they have changed about themselves, but don't say anything to your partner or ask him or her if you are right. Ready, turn!** Count to five out loud and then make sure all of the pairs have returned to their back-to-back positions.

Ask: **Who could tell what change their partner made? What was that change?** Give several of your students a chance to share. When everyone is finished sharing, have students sit down.

Explain: **We just learned how to be aware of very visible changes, but what about invisible things? Are we supposed to be aware of them also? What are some of the invisible things we should be aware of?** Give students a chance to share their ideas. Have one student read Hebrews 11:1. Make a transition to the Bible Exploration by saying: **According to Hebrews 11:1, faith means being sure of things, even if you can't see them. Today we're going to look at someone who had faith in what he could not see. Believe it or not, because of this faith, visible miracles happened.**

BIBLE EXPLORATION TWO (40 MINUTES)

Objective: To help students recall how Elisha demonstrated his faith in God.

Materials needed: Enough copies of "Gimme an E!" on page 37 for each student to have one, Bibles, paper, and pens or pencils, chalkboard, chalk and eraser; or white board and markers; or an overhead projector, transparency and markers.

Step 1: Ask: **Who can summarize the story of Elisha from last week? What did we learn about faith from this story?**

Step 2: Divide students into groups of three or four. Give each student a copy of "Gimme an E!" and a pen or pencil. Explain: **Today we're going to look at Elisha and how he had faith in God's presence. Work together as a group on the handout to think of a word or phrase that describes Elisha, beginning with each of the letters in his name.** Allow students to refer to 2 Kings 6:8-23.

Step 3: After six or seven minutes, ask for several responses to the following:
What were the two words that you circled to describe Elisha?
Why did you choose those two words?

Step 4: Have students remain in their small groups and give each group a sheet of paper. Explain: **Now pretend that you are Elisha and you are making a one-minute speech to the Israelites. Your speech must contain the following three elements** (write the following on the board or overhead transparency)**:**

    What happened today is...
    What we can learn about God is...
    This changes our lives because...

Work together as a group to write the speech and then choose a spokesperson to play the role of Elisha and read the speech to the entire group. After you have given each group seven or eight minutes, have each "Elisha" read his or her speech.

Step 5: Conclude by asking, **What were some of the key themes to these speeches? How do these themes cause a person's faith to grow?**

CONCLUSION AND DECISION (10 MINUTES)

Objective: To help students think about tangible ways they can trust in God this upcoming week.

Materials needed: Chalkboard, chalk and eraser; or white board and markers; or an overhead projector, transparency and markers.

Explain: **There are many things we trust in that are visible. What are some of those things?** Write students' answers on the board.

After giving students enough time to develop an extensive list, explain: **In the story of Elisha we see someone who trusted not just in the visible, but in the invisible God. Imagine if you couldn't trust in anything that was visible.** At this point, erase all that you have written on the board or overhead transparency. Remind students of Hebrews 11:1; read it aloud.

The truth is that God is the only thing we can completely trust in. What is one thing you can do to demonstrate your trust in God this week? Write their responses on the board or overhead.

Explain: **If you want to commit to actually trusting God in one of these ways this week, come up to the board (or overhead projector) and write your initials by that item.**

Close in prayer, asking God for strength to trust not in the visible but in the invisible.

THE WRITE STUFF

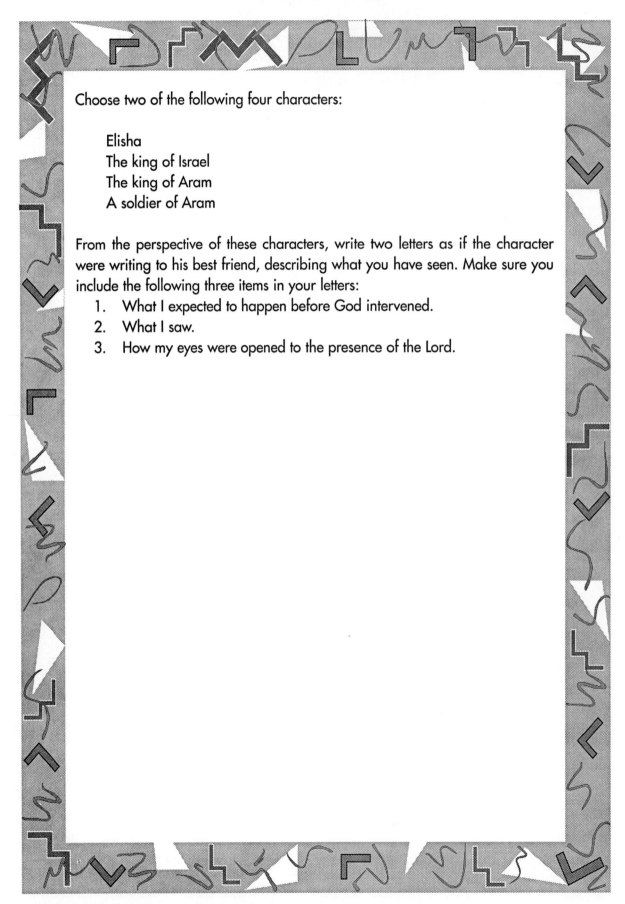

Choose two of the following four characters:

Elisha
The king of Israel
The king of Aram
A soldier of Aram

From the perspective of these characters, write two letters as if the character were writing to his best friend, describing what you have seen. Make sure you include the following three items in your letters:

1. What I expected to happen before God intervened.
2. What I saw.
3. How my eyes were opened to the presence of the Lord.

CONTINUED

Letter #1:

Dear friend,

Sincerely,

_____

Letter #2:

Dear friend,

Sincerely,

_____

GIMME AN E!

Now that you know more about the story of Elisha, work together as a group to come up with a word describing Elisha that begins with each of the letters in his name.

E
_____
_____

L
_____
_____

I
_____
_____

S
_____
_____

H
_____
_____

A
_____
_____

Circle the two most important qualities of these six characteristics.

Why did you choose those two qualities?

FOUR IN THE FIRE:

SHADRACH, MESHACH AND ABEDNEGO SERVE THE LORD

KEY VERSES

"Shadrach, Meshach and Abednego replied to the king, 'O Nebuchadnezzar, we do not need to defend ourselves before you in this matter. If we are thrown into the blazing furnace, the God we serve is able to save us from it, and he will rescue us from your hand, O king. But even if he does not, we want you to know, O king, that we will not serve your gods or worship the image of gold you have set up.'" Daniel 3:16-18

BIBLICAL BASIS

Daniel 3:1-30

FOCUS OF THE SESSION

Faith is acting in obedience to God in all situations.

AIMS OF THIS SESSION

During the session students will:

*   Examine the bold faith and obedience of Shadrach, Meshach and Abednego.
*   Understand their need to obey God in all situations.
*   Implement one or more practical and specific acts of obedience this week.

LEADER'S DEVOTIONAL

Recently, a New Jersey schoolteacher shared with his class the true story of a young woman who found $1,000. Instead of keeping the money for herself, she reported it lost.

The class's reaction to the woman's noble deed? All fifteen students labeled her a fool and criticized her for not keeping the money herself.

What's equally alarming about this story is that the teacher refrained from sharing his opinion about the woman's action. When asked why, the educator replied, "If I come from the position of what is right and wrong, then I'm their counselor."

Right and wrong. These two words are becoming more and more foreign to today's teenagers. For them, what is right is often synonymous with what is easy, or what works or what feels good. Wrong is what is hard or what demands a sacrifice.

This lesson on Shadrach, Meshach and Abednego gives you a chance to challenge students to think about what is right and wrong. What is right is what God asks us to do. What is wrong is doing the opposite. Once your students can differentiate between right and wrong, the key is to help them choose to *act* on what they know is right.

Faith requires action. Action requires obedience. Obedience, in turn, leads to more faith. In this lesson, your students will be challenged to think long and hard about a faith that works itself out in their every-day decisions. These little everyday decisions pave the way for a lifestyle of obedience in all decisions.

APPROACH THE WORD (15 MINUTES)

Objective: To provoke students' thinking about how they can decide who to obey.

Preparation and materials needed: Ahead of time, prepare several identical small paper bags and in each one place the following eight commands legibly written or typed on separate slips of paper:

> Cackle like a chicken for 10 seconds.
> Do four somersaults.
> Sing "Happy Birthday" to yourself.
> Twirl around like a ballerina five times.
> Fall to the ground and do three push-ups.
> Skip back to your team.
> Do 10 jumping jacks.
> Hop up and down 10 times.

Divide students into teams of four or five. Assign each team a paper bag containing the prepared commands, but then place the bags on the opposite end of the room. Explain, **Today we're going to do a relay race. When I say go, the first team member should run across the room and grab one command out of its bag and do what it says. When that person finishes that command, he or she runs back to the team. Then the second person runs across the room, grabs another command, finishes that command and returns so the next team member can go. There are eight commands total, so when your team has completed all eight raise your hands.**

After each team has finished, ask questions like these: **Why did you obey those commands? How did you feel about obeying these commands? In general, how do you know who you should obey?**

Make a transition to the next part of the session by saying something like this: **Today we're going to look at three young men who had to make a tough decision about who they were going to obey.**

BIBLE EXPLORATION (40 MINUTES)

Objective: To allow students to discover how an obedient example affects the faith of others.

Materials needed: One copy of "Four in the Fire" on pages 45-46, enough copies of "Whaddya Think About This Fire Thing?" on page 47 for each student to have one, Bibles and pens or pencils.

Step 1: Explain: **Today instead of just reading the Bible, we're also going to act out a story from it. I need ten volunteer actors.** If your group is smaller than ten students, ask some of the students to take on two roles. If your group is larger than ten students, ask the remaining students to be the audience and encourage the actors with their applause and cheers.

Assign each actor to be one of the biblical characters. As you read, pause to give the volunteers time to act out exactly what you have just read. Ask the rest of your students to serve as the audience to cheer for your actors.

Step 2: After the performance, give each student a copy of "Whaddya Think About This Fire Thing?" Without using their Bibles, have students decide if they agree or disagree with each of the four statements.

Step 3: Divide your students into groups of four or five. Make sure each group has at least one Bible, and explain: **Now we're going to look at the Bible itself to find the answers to these four questions. If you need to change your answer after you read the specific Scripture, feel free to do so.** Give them a few minutes to complete this activity.

Step 4: Bring the whole group together for a discussion of the following questions:

Which questions did you answer correctly the first time?

Which answers did you have to change once you read the Scriptures?

What other questions can you dream up about Shadrach, Meshach and Abednego?

Note: If you are completing this session in one meeting, ignore this break and continue with "Conclusion and Decision."

Two-Meeting Track: If you want to spread this session over two meetings, **STOP** here and close in prayer. Inform students of the content to be covered in your next meeting.

REVIEW AND APPROACH (15 MINUTES)

Objective: To trigger students' memories about the faith of Shadrach, Meshach and Abednego that they discussed during the last session.

Materials needed: Several packs of bubble gum, one paper plate for each team of four. Option: Instead of gum, play dough could be used.

Divide students into teams of four. Give each team one or two packs of bubble gum and a paper plate. Explain: **Today we're going to let you build your very own statues, but there's one catch: You get to build them out of your very own A.B.C. (Already Been Chewed) gum.**

Give students about a minute to chew their gum. Then say: **Now take your gum out of your mouth, and put it all together on your paper plate. Your team has four minutes to make a statue out of the gum you have chewed. The goal is to make it as tall as possible.**

Discuss: **Can you ever imagine commanding people to bow down to this statue? Why or why not?**
What do you remember from our last lesson?
How did Shadrach, Meshach and Abednego respond when they were forced to bow down to a statue?

BIBLE EXPLORATION TWO (40 MINUTES)

Objective: To help students understand the effects that their obedience and faith can have on others.

Materials needed: Enough copies of "The Faith Formula" on pages 48-50 and "My Friends and My Faith" on page 51 for each student to have one of each, Bibles and pens or pencils.

Step 1: Explain: **We see from Shadrach, Meshach and Abednego's story that when we obey God in all circumstances, our faith increases. Not only does our faith increase, but the faith of others also increases as they watch us obey God. Let's look at the various characters to see how Shadrach, Meshach and Abednego's obedience affected the faith of others.**

Divide students into groups of three or four. Give each student a copy of "The Faith Formula" along with a Bible and a pen or pencil. Ask each group to read Daniel 13:1-30 and then imagine how the various characters in the story were changed by Shadrach, Meshach and Abednego's obedience.

Step 2: After seven or eight minutes, ask:
Which characters stand out the most to you?
How was their faith increased?

Step 3: To encourage students to apply the truth that they too can influence their friends with their obedience, ask: **What do you think are the three most common areas in which your friends disobey God?** If students give several ideas, take a vote to narrow the list down to three areas of disobedience.

Step 4: Give each student a copy of "My Friends and My Faith." Give everyone a few minutes to complete the handout on their own.

CONCLUSION AND DECISION (20 MINUTES)

Objective: To allow students the opportunity to decide at least one way they can obey God this week.

Materials needed: Paper and pens or pencils.

Ask your students to return to their small groups of three or four. Explain: **We're going to give each group a paper and pen or pencil. Take five minutes to write out a brief case study that describes a tempting situation that would force a student to choose whether or not to obey God while he or she is at school. Make it as realistic as possible.**

When time is up, ask the groups to switch papers so each group has another group's case study. Say: **Now is your chance to respond to another group's case study. Take a few minutes to discuss how you would respond to the situation in the case study if you wanted to obey God.**

After five minutes, ask each group to share the case study they were given as well as their resolution to the dilemma.

Close in prayer, asking the Lord to give students the courage to obey God in all circumstances.

FOUR IN THE FIRE

ADAPTED FROM DANIEL 3

Characters:

King Nebuchadnezzar
The gold statue
Musician #1 (a trumpet player)
Musician #2 (a guitar player)
Shadrach
Meshach
Abednego
Soldier #1
Soldier #2
The fourth person in the fire

King Nebuchadnezzar was a very proud king. He liked to strut around his kingdom, flexing his muscles and saying to himself, "I am such a great king."

He thought he was such a good king that he built a gold statue. The gold statue stood tall and also looked very proud.

The entire kingdom was supposed to bow before the statue, but Shadrach, Meschach and Abednego refused to bow. When King Nebuchadnezzar heard this, he summoned them.

He shouted in their faces, "When you hear the musicians playing, you better bow to my statue. If not, I promise that I will throw you into the burning fire."

The musicians began to play. Shadrach, Meshach and Abednego shook their heads, refusing to bow. The king shouted in their faces, "Bow now." The musicians kept playing.

Shadrach, Meshach and Abednego kept shaking their heads and still refused to bow.

Nebuchadnezzar was hopping mad. Yes, he actually started to hop.

Shadrach told him, "Oh king, we know that God is able to save us from the fire and from you.

Meshach said, "Yeah."

Abednego added, "But even if He does not, we want you to know that we will not serve your gods or worship your gold image."

Meshach said, "Yeah."

CONTINUED

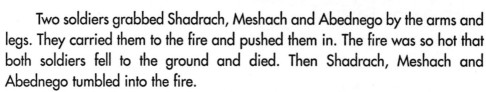

Two soldiers grabbed Shadrach, Meshach and Abednego by the arms and legs. They carried them to the fire and pushed them in. The fire was so hot that both soldiers fell to the ground and died. Then Shadrach, Meshach and Abednego tumbled into the fire.

The king looked into the fire and couldn't believe his eyes. He rubbed his eyes to make sure his vision was okay. His face looked shocked. "I can't believe it," he said, "Weren't there three men that we threw into the fire? Now I see four men walking around in the fire, and the fourth looks like a son of the gods."

Nebuchadnezzar shouted into the fire, "Shadrach, Meshach and Abednego, servants of the Most High God, come out of there!"

Shadrach, Meshach and Abednego walked out of the fire. Not a single hair was out of place or singed; their clothes were just fine.

Nebuchadnezzar proclaimed boldly, "Praise be to the God of Shadrach, Meshach and Abednego. They trusted in him and were willing to give up their lives rather than worship any god except their own God. Therefore I decree that this God is the true God." The two musicians began to play their instruments enthusiastically.

Shadrach, Meshach and Abednego hugged each other and jumped for joy for five more seconds as they shouted, "Yippee!"

The end.

WHADDYA THINK ABOUT THIS FIRE THING?

After you read each question, decide as a group whether you think the answer is true or false. Circle your answer.

1. When Shadrach, Meshach and Abednego decided not to bow but to obey God, they didn't know what it would cost them.

   True   False

2. Shadrach, Meshach and Abednego knew that God would protect them if they obeyed Him.

   True   False

3. The king knew that the fourth person in the fire was God.

   True   False

4. The king was convinced that Shadrach, Meshach and Abednego were obeying the true God.

   True   False

Once you've guessed on your own, look up the following Scriptures to see if your answers were right. Feel free to change your answer!

Question 1: Daniel 3:1-7
Question 2: Daniel 3:16-18
Question 3: Daniel 3:24-27
Question 4: Daniel 3:28-30

THE FAITH FORMULA

Describe how Shadrach, Meshach and Abednego's obedience increased the faith of the following people:

This person's faith was increased because...

Nebuchadnezzar

The musicians

CONTINUED

A friend of Shadrach, Meshach
and Abednego who saw what happened

The people who heated
up the furnace

CONTINUED

The family of the guards
who were killed

The entire kingdom

MY FRIENDS AND MY FAITH

In the first column, write the three biggest areas in which you see your friends disobey God.

In the second, write what you can do to obey God in this area.

Then list how your obedience could help your friends learn about God in the third column.

How My Friends Disobey God	How I Could Obey God	How My Obedience Can Help My Friends Learn About God
1.		
2.		
3.		

WRONG-WAY JONAH:

GOD SAVES NINEVEH

KEY VERSE

"Salvation comes from the LORD." Jonah 2:9

BIBLICAL BASIS

Jonah 1—4

FOCUS OF THE SESSION

Faith is knowing that God loves and accepts all people.

AIMS OF THIS SESSION

During this session, students will:
*   Examine Jonah's struggle in caring for the Ninevites;
*   Discover the importance of showing love to all people;
*   Implement a practical way in which to show God's love to someone during the coming week.

LEADER'S DEVOTIONAL

There is probably no social hierarchy that is as strict and well-defined as in the junior-high culture. There are the popular kids. Then there are the band kids, the smart kids, the party kids, the jock kids, the skater kids, the surfer kids, the nerdy kids and the list goes on. Each group has its own preferred style of dress, its own music, its own slang and its own way of life. Because of this, junior highers often develop tunnel vision. Whether they are at school, in their neighborhood or even at church, they become so myopic in their focus on their own particular identity group that they lose sight of individuality—who each of them is as a unique creation of God.

This lesson shatters the group mentality by reminding students that God loves and accepts *all* people. It doesn't matter how they dress or talk or what kind of music they listen to—God still loves them. For the more popular students, this brings a sense of responsibility as they realize that they are to reach out to others, even (and maybe even especially) the less popular kids. For the most insecure students, this brings freedom as they realize that they are loved just as they are. In a world full of comparisons and labels, God's love is blind to all human categories.

APPROACH THE WORD (10 MINUTES)

Objective: To help students understand that God loves all people equally.

Preparation and materials needed: Ahead of time, cut out pictures of people from newspapers or magazines. The people portrayed should be a diverse cross section of humanity, from politicians to athletes, from elderly to children.

Explain: **Today we're going to look at God's love for people.** Show the pictures to the class one at a time. After students have seen all of the pictures, ask: **Which of these people do you think God loves the most?** Let the whole group discuss who God loves the most. Of course, this is a trick question, because the correct answer is that God loves all people equally.

Explain: **The truth is that God loves all people equally. Look at the person sitting to your left; now look at the person sitting to your right. God loves each of you equally.**

Make a transition to the lesson by explaining: **Today we're going to look at how Jonah learned the hard way that God loves all people equally.**

BIBLE EXPLORATION (40 MINUTES)

Objective: To give students an in-depth look at God's love and care for all people in the story of Jonah.

Materials needed: Enough copies of "To Care or Not to Care" on pages 59-60 for each student to have one, pens or pencils, paper, and Bibles.

Step 1: Divide your group into at least four small groups, even if the groups are only two or three students apiece. Explain: **We're going to look at the amazing story of Jonah to see how God cares for all people.** Pass out pens or pencils, paper and Bibles and assign a chapter of Jonah to each group. Explain: **Now that you have chosen your chapter, read that chapter aloud in your group and choose two verses that you feel capture what is happening in that chapter. Write out the two verses you have selected.**

Step 2: After five to seven minutes, ask each group to read its chosen verses aloud. Ask each group to share: **Why did you select those two verses?**

Step 3: Distribute the "To Care or Not to Care" handout and a pen or pencil to each student. Say: **In your groups, fill out the handout, trac-**

ing the times when Jonah seemed to care and those times when he didn't seem to care.

Step 4: Give students 20 minutes to complete the handout, then ask: **How did you paraphrase God's words to Jonah in chapter 4? After God's rebuke, do you think Jonah ended up caring or not caring about the people of Nineveh?**

Note: If you are completing this session in one meeting, ignore this break and continue with "Conclusion and Decision."

Two-Meeting Track: If you want to spread this session over two meetings, **STOP** here and close in prayer. Inform students of the content to be covered in your next meeting.

REVIEW AND APPROACH (10 MINUTES)

Objective: To help students think about God's equal love for all people.

Materials needed: Enough copies of "Your Favorite Fives" on pages 61-64 for each student to have one and pens or pencils.

Explain: **Today we're going to discover some of your favorite things.** As you pass out copies of " Your Favorite Fives" handout and pens or pencils to your students, tell them: **Complete these questions by writing your favorite five things in each of the categories.**

Give students five minutes to complete the handout, then ask: **Who would like to share your five favorite foods? What about your five favorite television shows? How about your five favorite fun things to do?**

How about God's five favorite people? Explain: **Actually, this question is a trick question. God doesn't play favorites. He loves each one of us, and each person in the world, equally.**

Make a transition to the lesson by explaining: **Today we're going to see how Jonah learned through some difficult experiences that God loves all people equally.**

Bible Exploration Two (40 Minutes)

Materials needed: Enough copies of "Wrong-Way Joey" on pages 65-66 for each student to have one, pens or pencils, paper, Bibles, and enough envelopes and postage stamps for each student to have one.

Step 1: Divide students into groups of three or four. Distribute copies of "Wrong-Way Joey" handouts and pens or pencils to each group. Explain: **Let's see what Jonah's life would be like if he were a junior higher who lived in your neighborhood and attended your school. We'll call him "Wrong-Way Joey."**

Continue to explain: **Work together as a group to complete the first sentence. Then switch handouts with another group. Now your group completes the second sentence of the handout keeping in mind the information that's already written on the sheet. After completing that sentence, switch papers again with another group. Keep doing this until you've completed all six sentences.**

Step 2: After twenty minutes, ask the small groups to read the stories they have written.

Step 3: Discuss:

Have you ever felt like Joey?

What do you feel God might want you to be doing right now?

Step 4: Explain: **Often the toughest group to show tangible love to is our families. I'm going to give you a piece of paper, a pen(cil), an envelope and a stamp. On the paper, write a letter to one of your family members. You can choose a parent, a brother, a sister, a grandparent, an aunt, an uncle—anyone in your family that you feel you need to show love to today. Let them know how much you love them and mention specific things about them that you appreciate. This letter may be the perfect opportunity for you to apologize to someone for saying something mean, being disobedient or causing some other conflict.**

Give your students about seven minutes to do this, encouraging them to be as specific as possible. Then explain: **Now you need to put your letter inside your envelope, address it and put a stamp on it. We'll mail it for you. If you don't know the person's address, you can just hand it to them or mail it yourself once you find out his or her address.**

Conclusion and Decision (20 Minutes)

Objective: To help students specifically choose one way they can show God's love and care for another person during the coming week.

Materials needed: Enough copies of "Caring on the Campus" on pages 67-68 for each student to have one and pens or pencils.

Explain: **Since God loves all people, we should do likewise and love all people. Right now we have the chance to think about a few specific actions we can take to love others this week.**

Distribute a copy of "Caring on the Campus" handout to each student. Explain: **Please draw a map of the lunch area on your campus. Include not just the buildings, but also people who tend to hang out in certain areas.** Give students five minutes to draw the campus map.

Explain: **Now I want you to make a list at the bottom of your handout of people you feel that you have showed love to in the past month and how you showed that love.** After a few minutes, have a few students share some of the names they listed and how they showed love to those people in the past month.

Explain: **Now on the bottom of your handout make a second list. This time list two or three people you can show love to during this next week and how you will show love to them. Make the way you show love to them as tangible and specific as you possibly can.** Give them concrete examples, such as eating lunch with a newcomer, complimenting someone who seems to have inferior feelings about him- or herself, etc.

After giving them a few minutes to complete the list, lead students in prayer, asking God to help them show tangible love to others this week. Then give them a time for silent personal prayer.

ALTERNATE CONCLUSION (20 MINUTES)

Objective: To help students work together to show God's love to others in their church, neighborhood or school.

Have a time of group brainstorming for ideas to show love to someone in the church, neighborhood or on their school campus(es). List the ideas on the board, flip chart or overhead. Some examples might include: doing yard work for an elderly church member, giving a young mother a free afternoon by watching her small children, paying for a homeless person's meal, honoring a teacher at school by sending him or her flowers and a thank-you note, etc.

After about ten minutes of brainstorming, have the whole group or smaller groups of students choose one way they can show God's love for someone from the listed ideas. Give them a few minutes to plan when and how they will implement their idea.

Meet with students who participate in this group activity later in the week or just before the next session to discuss what they did and what the results were.

TO CARE OR NOT TO CARE

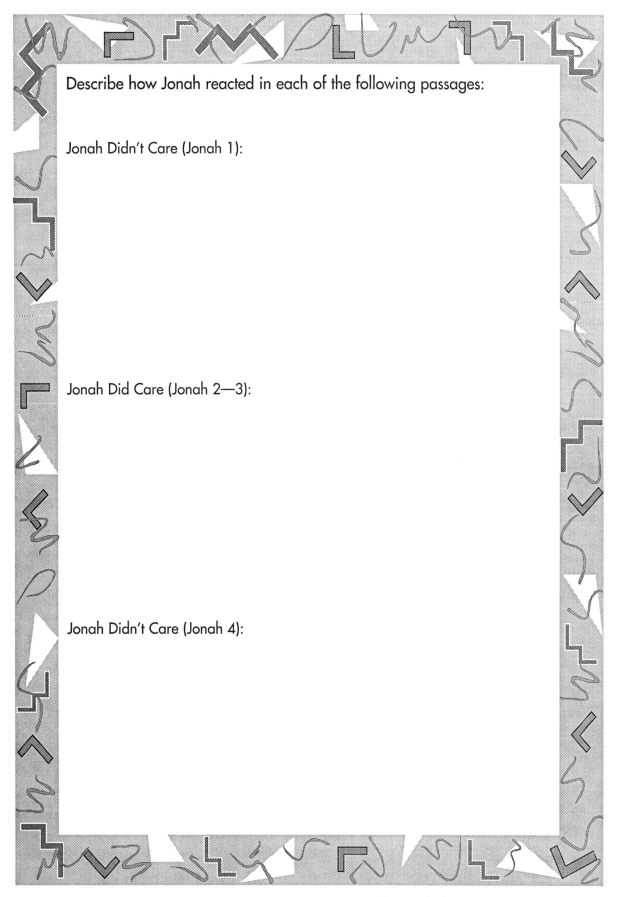

Describe how Jonah reacted in each of the following passages:

Jonah Didn't Care (Jonah 1):

Jonah Did Care (Jonah 2—3):

Jonah Didn't Care (Jonah 4):

CONTINUED

How would you paraphase God's rebuke to Jonah 4:10,11 in your own words?

After God's rebuke, do you think Jonah cared or didn't care about the people of Nineveh? Why or why not?

YOUR FAVORITE FIVES

List your favorite five things in each category. Be creative!

YOUR FAVORITE FIVE FOODS

1.

2.

3.

4.

5.

CONTINUED

YOUR FAVORITE FIVE TELEVISION SHOWS

1.

2.

3.

4.

5.

CONTINUED

YOUR FAVORITE FIVE FUN THINGS TO DO

1.

2.

3.

4.

5.

CONTINUED

GOD'S FAVORITE FIVE PEOPLE

1.

2.

3.

4.

5.

WRONG-WAY JOEY

Let's see what Jonah's life would be like if he was a junior higher who lived in your neighborhood and attended your school. We'll call him "Wrong-Way Joey."

As a group, work together to complete sentence number one. Then switch handouts with another group so that you complete sentence number two, keeping in mind the information already written on the page. After completing that sentence, switch papers again with another group. Keep doing this until you've completed all six sentences.

1. Wrong-Way Joey feels God calling him to...

2. Joey doesn't want to because...

3. God teaches him by...

4. Because God used Joey, many people decided to...

5. Joey gets frustrated because...

6. God tells Joey...

CARING ON THE CAMPUS

Draw a map of your campus at lunch, including buildings and people who normally hang out at various locations.

CONTINUED

1. People who I've shown love to this past month:

   _____   _____   _____

2. People who I'd like to show   What I'll do:
   love to this week:

   _____   _____

   _____   _____

   _____   _____

WITHOUT A DOUBT:

JESUS IS ALIVE!

KEY VERSES

"For God so loved the world that he gave his one and only Son, that whoever believes in him shall not perish but have eternal life." John 3:16

BIBLICAL BASIS

John 3:16; 20:1-31; Romans 3:23; 6:23

FOCUS OF THE SESSION

Faith is receiving God's love and forgiveness.

AIMS OF THIS SESSION

During this session, students will:

- Examine the evidence of Jesus' resurrection;
- Discover their need to accept the truth of Jesus' resurrection;
- Accept the gift of salvation Jesus offers.

LEADER'S DEVOTIONAL

"I'd love Jesus even if He wasn't true."

At first glance, this real statement from a contemporary Christian leader might sound noble, but read it again. It's actually alarming. In an age of relativism, we as Christians must be dedicated to Jesus not just because of our own emotional experience but because of our intellectual examination of the facts.

The facts proving Jesus' resurrection are staggering. In this lesson, your students get to play the role of a judge examining the evidence before they eventually decide whether or not Jesus is alive.

If the resurrection isn't true, it's time to stop playing church and find better ways to spend our time.

If the resurrection is true, it's time for you, your students and your youth ministry to begin the adventure of a radically changed Christian lifestyle.

APPROACH TO THE WORD (10 MINUTES)

Objective: To help students begin to think about what the truth really is.

Preparation needed: Write down two truthful statements and one false statement about yourself. Choose statements that your students wouldn't know or even guess about you.

Explain: **Today we're going to look at whether or not Jesus' resurrection is true. But first, I'm wondering if you can tell what the truth is about me and each other. We're going to play the game "Two Truths and a Lie." I will share two truths about myself and one lie. You have to try to figure out which are the truthful statements and which is the false one.** Read aloud the three statements about yourself. Then reread each statement, pausing after each one to ask students to raise their hands if they think that statement is a lie.

Now ask: **What about you? Can anyone tell us two truths and one lie about him- or herself?** (You may want to ask some students to be prepared ahead of time with two truths and one lie.)

After a few students have shared and other students have guessed which of the three statements is the lie, make a transition to the Bible Exploration by saying: **Today we're going to look at the true story about Jesus. At the end of our time together, you're going to have a chance to decide whether or not you think the story is true and what your response will be.**

BIBLE EXPLORATION (45 MINUTES)

Objective: To challenge students to examine the evidence about Jesus' crucifixion and resurrection.

Materials needed: Enough copies of "You Be the Judge" handout on pages 75-77 for each student to have one, pens or pencils, and Bibles.

Step 1: Explain: **Today we've got a very exciting passage of Scripture to read. It's all about what happened to Jesus after He died.** Make sure each student has a Bible and then explain: **We need some volunteers to read John 20:1-31. Who wants to begin?**

Step 2: After you've finished reading John 20, explain: **Today you're going to be the judge about the evidence surrounding Jesus' death.** Divide students into groups of three. Give each student a copy of the "You Be the Judge" handout and a pen or pencil. Tell them: **Work together as a group to list all of the evidence the Bible gives about Jesus' crucifixion and resurrection. Even though you work in a group, make sure that each of you writes down all of the evidence you find.**

Step 3: After 20 minutes, ask: **What are some of the most important pieces of evidence about Jesus?** Give students plenty of time to share what they think are the most important pieces of evidence about Jesus' death and resurrection.

Step 4: Explain: **Given all the evidence you have just heard and read, what do you think? If you were a judge in this case, what would be your verdict? Do you think there is enough evidence to prove that Jesus is in fact the crucified and resurrected son of God? At the bottom of your handout, write out your verdict.**

Note: If you are completing this session in one meeting, ignore this break and continue with "Conclusion and Decision."

Two-Meeting Track: If you want to spread this session over two meetings, STOP here and close in prayer. Collect the "You Be the Judge" handouts from student so you'll have them for your next session. Inform students of the content to be covered in your next meeting.

REVIEW AND APPROACH (10 MINUTES)

Objective: To help students review the evidence about Jesus' crucifixion and resurrection that they examined in the last session.

Materials needed: A gift-wrapped package.

Explain: **During the last session, we looked at the available evidence of Jesus' death and resurrection. What do you remember about that evidence?** Give students a few minutes to recall the evidence.

Say: **Jesus' death and resurrection made new life possible for us. It's like this gift** (hold up the gift as you are talking). **How many of you like getting gifts? What's the best gift you've ever received?**

Well, believe it or not, the gift of salvation that Jesus offers is a thousand times better than any other gift you've ever received. At the end of today you'll have a chance to choose whether or not to accept that gift.

BIBLE EXPLORATION TWO (40 MINUTES)

Objective: To examine the evidence of Jesus' resurrection and allow students to come to a point of decision about the truth of Jesus' resurrection.

Materials needed: The copies of "You Be the Judge" student handout from the previous session, pens or pencils, and paper.

Step 1: Explain: **Today we're going to look even closer at the evidence surrounding Jesus' resurrection. I'm going to return your "You Be the Judge" handouts that you completed last time.** As you pass them out, continue to explain: **If you weren't here, make sure you are sitting next to someone who was so that you can read his or her "You Be the Judge" handout. I'm going to divide you up into two teams: the prosecution and the defense. Using John 20, the prosecution team will present the evidence for the resurrection, and the defense team will ask questions of the prosecution.**

Give each group paper and pens or pencils so that they can organize their evidence or their questions. Give the groups 8 to 10 minutes to get organized. Encourage them to be as creative as possible using witnesses and/or props. You may want to select the "attorney" representative for each group who will lead their team's part of the discussion.

Step 2: Ask the prosecution team to present its evidence. As the leader, you will take the part of the "judge" and moderate and steer the discussion as needed.

Step 3: After the prosecution has presented its evidence, ask the defense team to ask the questions they've prepared.

Step 4: At the end of the defense questions, ask both teams: **If your side was the one who presented the truth, what difference would that make in your life?**

CONCLUSION AND DECISION (10 MINUTES)

Objective: To give students the amazing opportunity to accept God's love and forgiveness.

Materials needed: Several pieces of ribbon approximately six inches long, or have a spool of ribbon and a pair of scissors so that you can cut off a piece of ribbon as each student responds.

Explain: **Now that you've had a chance to look at the evidence, what do you think? Is it true?**

The most well-known verse in the Bible is John 3:16. It says, "For God so loved the world that He gave His one and only Son, that whoever believes in him shall not perish but have eternal life."

Let's highlight three truths in this verse:

First, God loves the world. As we saw with the story of Jonah, He loves all people—including you.

Second, God sent His son Jesus to the earth. Even the history books agree that a man named Jesus Christ walked on earth. God sent Jesus because of our sin which separates us from God.

"For all have sinned and fall short of the glory of God" (Romans 3:23). "For the wages of sin is death, but the gift of God is eternal life in Christ Jesus our Lord." (Romans 6:23).

Third, you and I can have eternal life, but we must believe in Jesus and ask Him to take control of our lives.

Do you believe that today? Will you ask Jesus to be your Savior and Lord, to come and take control of your life?

Jesus offers you the free gift of salvation to save you from your sin and to give you eternal life. This decision is the most important choice you will ever make. It's more important than your choice of a spouse or even your career choice. Do you want to choose Jesus today?

Close your eyes and bow your heads and pray silently. Give them a minute, then say: If you have never before made a public commitment to accept Jesus Christ's gift of salvation, open your eyes, stand up, and come forward and take a piece of this gift ribbon as a sign that you are receiving the gift of salvation. You can then return to your seats.

After students have come forward for their pieces of ribbon, lead them in the following prayer. Have them silently repeat after you, pausing at each ellipsis (…):

> **Dear Jesus…,**
>   **I know that I have sinned…and that I need**
> **you…. Please come into my life…and be my Lord**
> **and Savior…. I turn control of my life over to you….**
> **Amen….**

Note to leader: Please be prepared to follow-up on the students making this decision.

YOU BE THE JUDGE

Read John 20:1-31 and write down all the evidence you find that indicates Jesus really was resurrected after His death. (Hint: You should be able to find at least nine things!)

1.

2.

3.

CONTINUED

4.

5.

6.

7.

CONTINUED

8.

9.

After all this evidence, what is your verdict?

   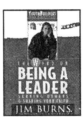   

Youth Ministry Resources from Gospel Light.

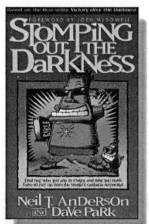

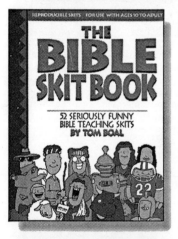